The SAMHAIN SEASON JOURNAL

by Trixie Freebird & Jechanovia

Copyright © 2021 by Trixie Freebird & Jechanovia
All rights reserved.

This book or any portion thereof may not be
reproduced or used in any manner whatsoever
without express written permission of the authors.

www.magicked.ca

SEASON OF SAMHAIN

FLORA

Tansy, chrysanthemum, echinacea, dried grass

CRYSTALS

Obsidian, Bloodstone, Smoky Quartz, Onyx, Carnelian, Black Tourmaline

ESSENTIAL OILS

Bay Laurel, Clary Sage, Black Pepper, Oak Moss

FOODS

Pumpkins, squash, apples, carrots, potatoes, beets, brussels sprouts

DEITIES

Cerridwen, Cailleach, Persephone, Cernunnos, Dionysus, Aradia, Morrigan, Lilith

SYMBOLS

Cauldron, moon, seeds, pentagram, besom, acorn,

SCORPIO ARCHETYPE

Scorpio • Scorpion
October 23–November 22

Ruled by Mars & Pluto
Element of Water • Quality is Fixed

Scorpios are extremely deep people who can not stand anything shallow or inauthentic. They are emotional, intellectual, assertive and competitive. This sign is known for its intensity as well as it's passionate and highly sensual nature. Scorpios are determined and driven by success, making them natural leaders. Beware the sting of the scorpion if you upset or anger one.

When balanced: Honest, Loyal, Ambitious, Courageous, Determined
When unbalanced: Controlling, Jealous, Resentful, Harsh, Secretive

SEASON OF SAMHAIN

SPELLWORK

Black Salt Recipe

Dead Sea Salt
Charcoal from a sacred fire
Ground Egg shells
Star Anise
Black Peppercorns
Cloves
Myrrh essential oil

ALTAR MAGICK

Pumpkins, cloves, cinnamon, coriander, star anise, vanilla, dried flowers, mirrors, ancestral photos, heirlooms, black cloth, toadstool,

"Go collect weird shit from ditches, witches. Good shit grows in ditches."
~ *Trixie Freebird*

SAGITTARIUS ARCHETYPE

Sagittarius • Archer
November 23-December 21

Ruled by Jupiter
Element of Fire • Quality is Mutable

Sagittarius is the sign that unequivocally follows the beat of their own drum and has a driving quest for growth, adventure and freedom. Sagittarius individuals are fun loving and socially driven people. Sagittarius are both intellectual and emotionally intelligent. They are often some of the best communicators, conversationalists and debaters with a never ending thirst for knowledge. Sag is often known as the philosopher and spiritual teacher.

When balanced: Kind, Compassionate, Optimistic, Spontaneous, Innovative and Independent
When unbalanced: Bored Easily, Fears commitment, Stubborn, and Egoic

SEASON OF SAMHAIN

JECHANOVIA'S PUMPKIN SPICED CHAI LATTE

1 can evaporated milk or milk substitute
6 – 8 cups water
2 tbsp loose black tea or (3 teabags)
1 – 2 cinnamon sticks
6 – 10 whole cloves
2 – 4 whole star anise
1 cup canned pumpkin
1/2 – 1 cup brown sugar or honey

1. mix all ingredients in a large pot or slow cooker, then heat over medium-low, stirring often until hot and tea has steeped to taste.

2. ladle into mugs and serve.

adapted from The Kitchen Magick Cookbook

TRIXIE'S SAMHAIN STEW

4 garlic cloves minced
2 onions chopped
2 shallots chopped
2 tsp ground cinnamon
2 tsp ground cumin
1 tsp ground coriander
½ tsp cayenne pepper
½ tsp ground allspice
¼ tsp salt

3 cups water
3 veggie broth cubes
2 large sweet potatoes cubed
1 can chickpeas
4 carrots chopped
4 celery stocks chopped
1 bulb fennel chopped
1 large can of tomato sauce
1 ½ cups pumpkin

Cook cloves, onion and shallot in olive oil. Add vegetables, cook and stir over medium heat until softened. Add water and veggie broth cubes and combine. Add tomato sause and pumpkin. Reduce heat to medium-low and continue to simmer until thoroughly hot. Feeds 5 – 8 people.

SEASON OF SAMHAIN

SAMHAIN CARD SPREAD

CARD 1: Embrace

CARD 2: Release

CARD 3: Shadow work

CARD 4: Celebrate

NOTES FOR SAMHAIN SPREAD

OCTOBER 31ST
• Blessed Samhain •

MY SPELLS **MY ALTAR**

MY TRADITIONS

OCTOBER 31ST
• Blessed Samhain •

JOURNAL

DATE:

TODAY'S GOALS   DAILY DIVINATION

I'M GRATEFUL FOR...   TODAY, I'M FEELING...

DATE:

JOURNAL

DATE:

TODAY

DAILY DIVINATION

GRATITUDE LIST

DATE:

JOURNAL

DATE:

TODAY

DAILY DIVINATION

GRATITUDE LIST

DATE:

JOURNAL

DATE:

TODAY   DAILY DIVINATION

GRATITUDE LIST

DATE:

JOURNAL

DATE:

TODAY   DAILY DIVINATION

GRATITUDE LIST

DATE:

JOURNAL

DATE:

TODAY   DAILY DIVINATION

GRATITUDE LIST

DATE:

JOURNAL

DATE:

TODAY   DAILY DIVINATION

GRATITUDE LIST

DATE:

JOURNAL

DATE:

TODAY **DAILY DIVINATION**

GRATITUDE LIST

DATE:

JOURNAL

DATE:

TODAY						DAILY DIVINATION

GRATITUDE LIST

DATE:

JOURNAL

DATE:

TODAY   DAILY DIVINATION

GRATITUDE LIST

DATE:

JOURNAL

DATE:

TODAY   DAILY DIVINATION

GRATITUDE LIST

DATE:

JOURNAL

DATE:

TODAY   DAILY DIVINATION

GRATITUDE LIST

DATE:

JOURNAL

DATE:

TODAY   DAILY DIVINATION

GRATITUDE LIST

DATE:

JOURNAL

DATE:

TODAY   DAILY DIVINATION

GRATITUDE LIST

DATE:

JOURNAL

DATE:

TODAY   DAILY DIVINATION

GRATITUDE LIST

DATE:

JOURNAL

DATE:

TODAY   DAILY DIVINATION

GRATITUDE LIST

DATE:

JOURNAL

DATE:

TODAY   DAILY DIVINATION

GRATITUDE LIST

DATE:

JOURNAL

DATE:

TODAY   DAILY DIVINATION

GRATITUDE LIST

DATE:

JOURNAL

DATE:

TODAY   DAILY DIVINATION

GRATITUDE LIST

DATE:

JOURNAL

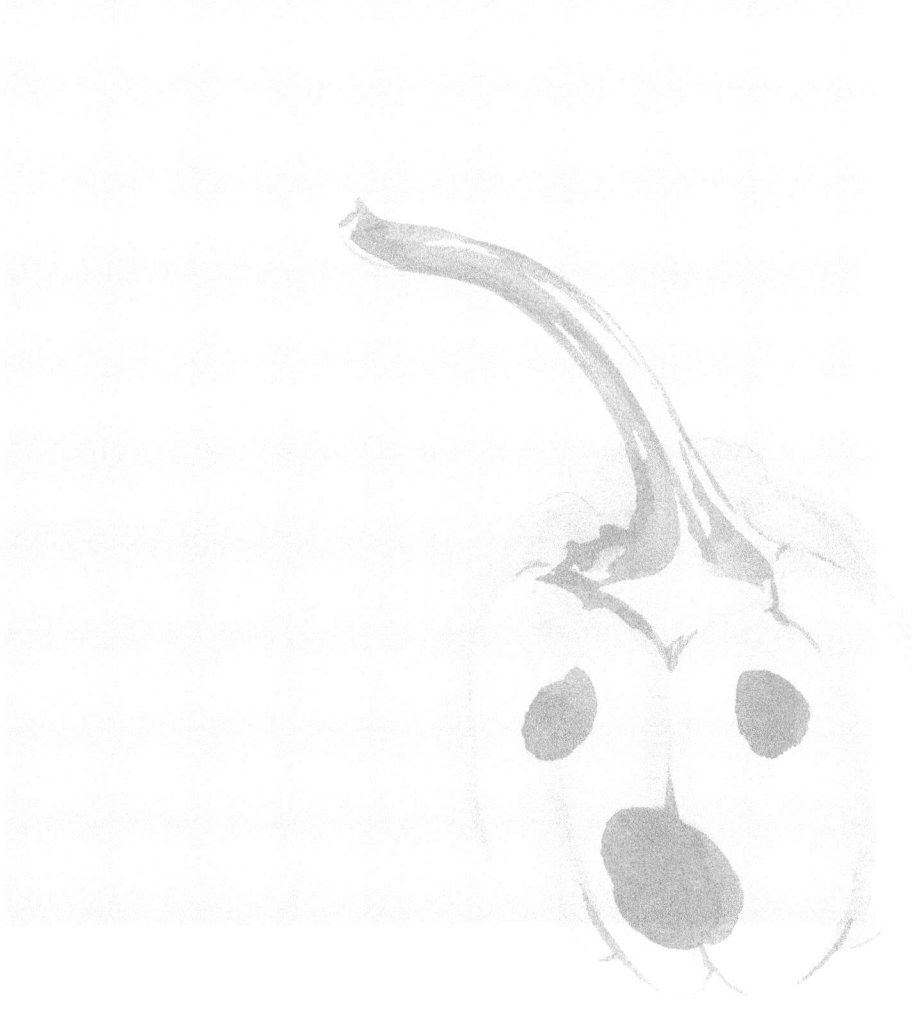

DATE:

TODAY   DAILY DIVINATION

GRATITUDE LIST

DATE:

JOURNAL

DATE:

TODAY   DAILY DIVINATION

GRATITUDE LIST

DATE:

JOURNAL

DATE:

TODAY   DAILY DIVINATION

GRATITUDE LIST

DATE:

JOURNAL

DATE:

TODAY   DAILY DIVINATION

GRATITUDE LIST

DATE:

JOURNAL

DATE:

TODAY   DAILY DIVINATION

GRATITUDE LIST

DATE:

JOURNAL

DATE:

TODAY   DAILY DIVINATION

GRATITUDE LIST

DATE:

JOURNAL

DATE:

TODAY

DAILY DIVINATION

GRATITUDE LIST

DATE:

JOURNAL

DATE:

TODAY   DAILY DIVINATION

GRATITUDE LIST

DATE:

JOURNAL

DATE:

TODAY

DAILY DIVINATION

GRATITUDE LIST

DATE:

JOURNAL

DATE:

TODAY   DAILY DIVINATION

GRATITUDE LIST

DATE:

JOURNAL

DATE:

TODAY   **DAILY DIVINATION**

GRATITUDE LIST

DATE:

JOURNAL

DATE:

TODAY   DAILY DIVINATION

GRATITUDE LIST

DATE:

JOURNAL

DATE:

TODAY   DAILY DIVINATION

GRATITUDE LIST

DATE:

JOURNAL

DATE:

TODAY   DAILY DIVINATION

GRATITUDE LIST

DATE:

JOURNAL

DATE:

TODAY

DAILY DIVINATION

GRATITUDE LIST

DATE:

JOURNAL

DATE:

TODAY   DAILY DIVINATION

GRATITUDE LIST

DATE:

JOURNAL

DATE:

TODAY   DAILY DIVINATION

GRATITUDE LIST

DATE:

JOURNAL

DATE:

TODAY   DAILY DIVINATION

GRATITUDE LIST

DATE:

JOURNAL

DATE:

TODAY   DAILY DIVINATION

GRATITUDE LIST

DATE:

JOURNAL

DATE:

TODAY   DAILY DIVINATION

GRATITUDE LIST

DATE:

JOURNAL

DATE:

TODAY

DAILY DIVINATION

GRATITUDE LIST

DATE:

JOURNAL

DATE:

TODAY   DAILY DIVINATION

GRATITUDE LIST

DATE:

JOURNAL

DATE:

TODAY   DAILY DIVINATION

GRATITUDE LIST

DATE:

JOURNAL

ABOUT TRIXIE

Trixie is a solitary Witch that follows the old ways, traditions and Wheel of the Year. She celebrates the Sabbats with joy, reverence and devotion to the Craft. Trixie is a lifelong student of esoterics and metaphysics. When she's not working with plant medicines and botanical aromatherapy, she spends her time creating art, sound and crystal healing, practicing divination, gardening, and kitchen witchery.

Learn more about Trixie at www.trixiefreebird.ca, and visit her shop at www.freebirdapothecary.ca. Follow her on Instagram @trixie.freebird.

ABOUT JECHANOVIA

Jechanovia is a sovereign Pagan Druid who loves to wander barefoot through the forest, cuddle baby chickens, and talk Tarot. The celebration of the Wheel of the Year is a sacred part of Jechanovia's spiritual practice. A lover of history, tradition, and the Earth Herself, she is always seeking out the magicks within the mundane.

Learn more about Jechanovia and her work at www.jechanovia.com, and connect with her on Instagram @iamjechanovia.

Lightning Source UK Ltd.
Milton Keynes UK
UKHW051916121022
410367UK00010B/255